I Go!

by Tammy Jones

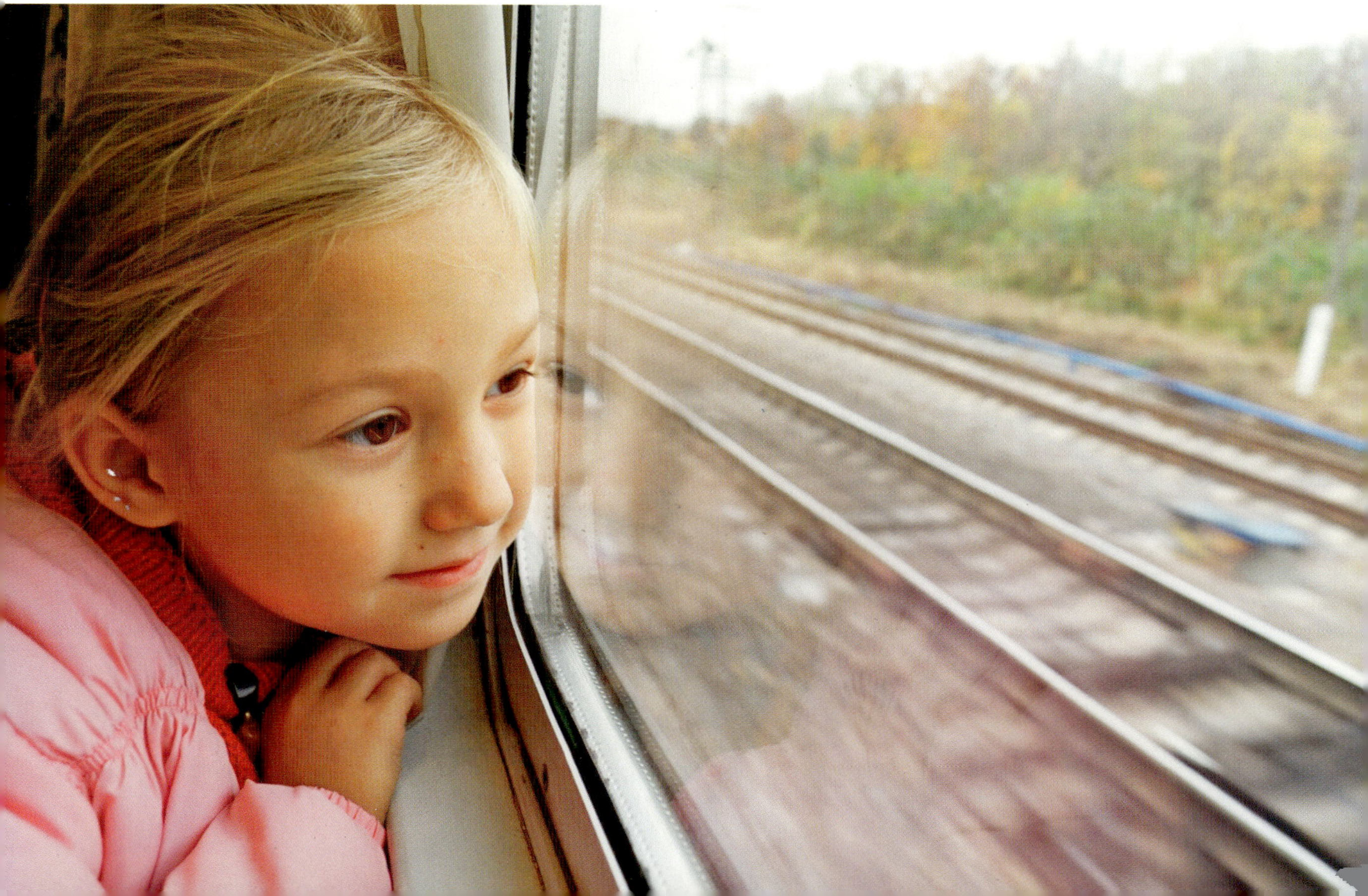

Picture Words

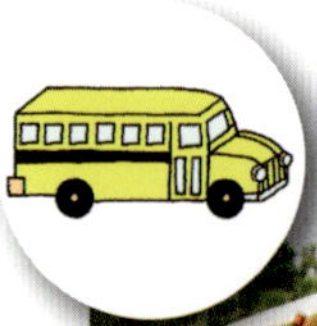

bus

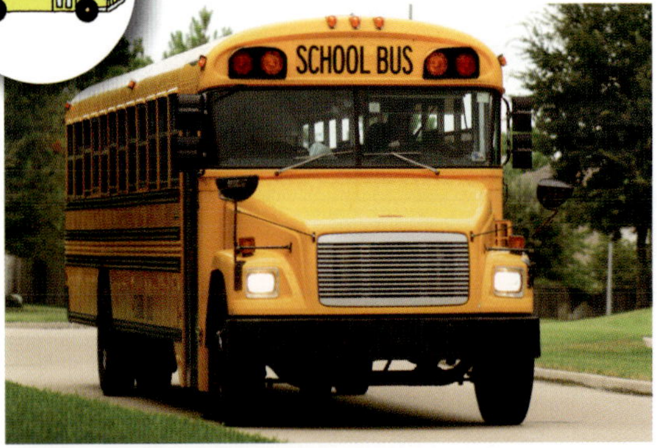

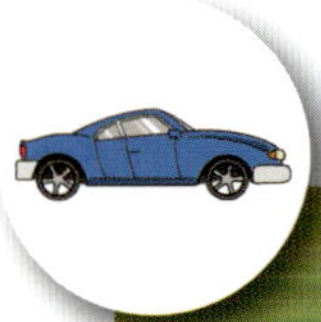

car

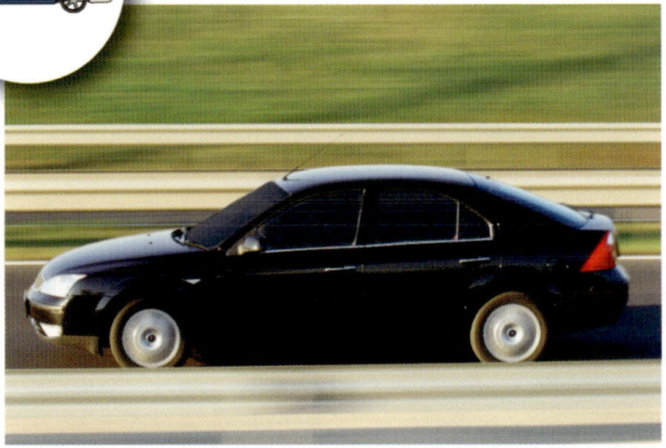

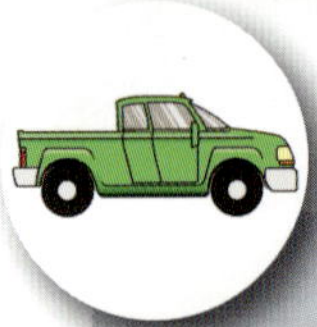

truck

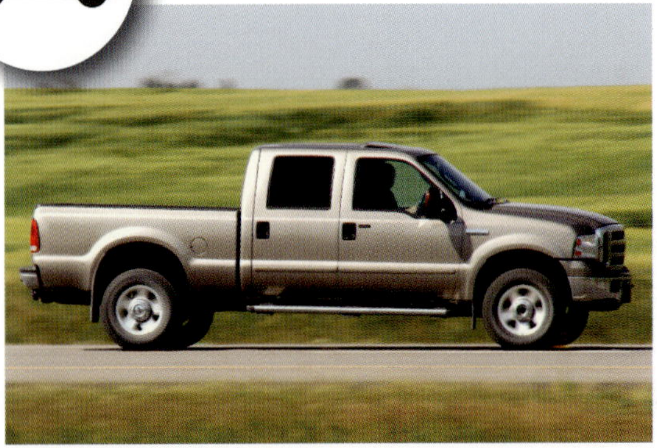

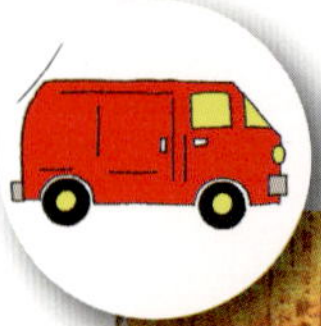

van

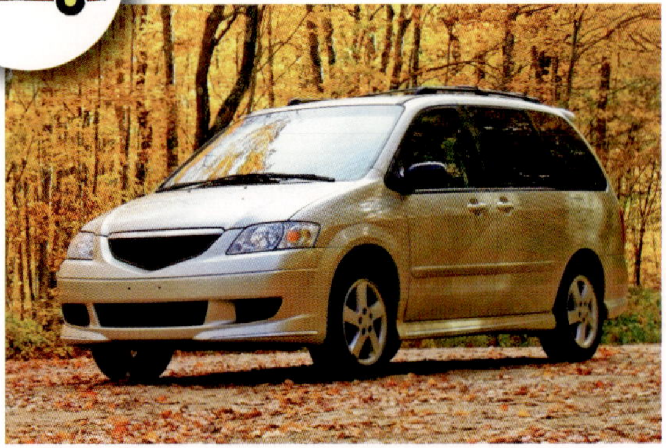

Sight Words

a

go

I

in

I go in a 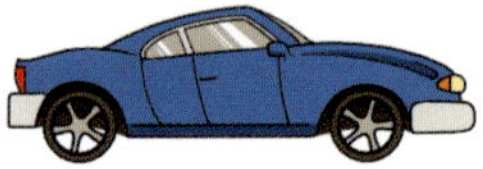 .

car

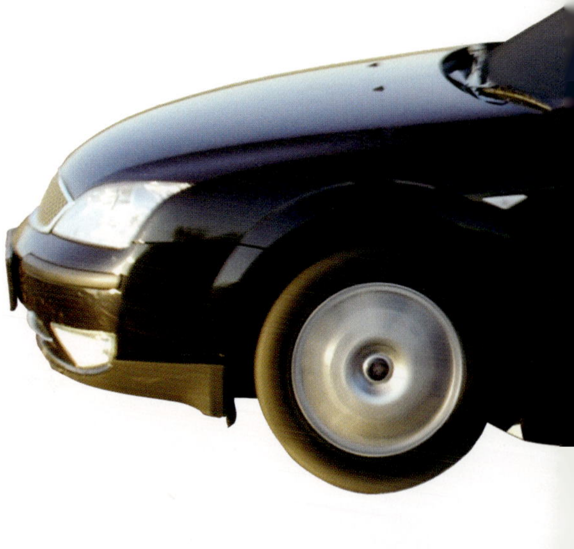

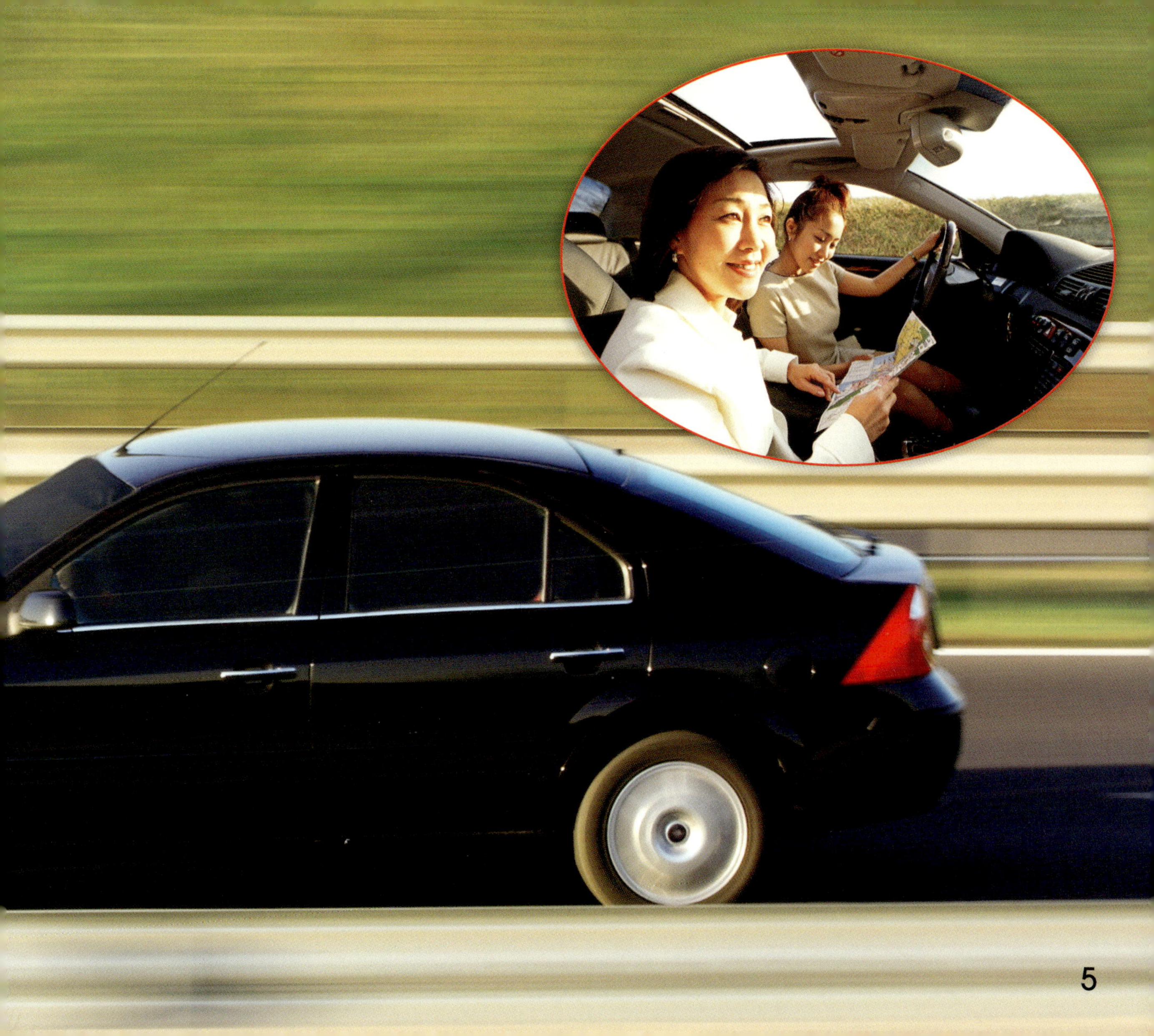

I go in a 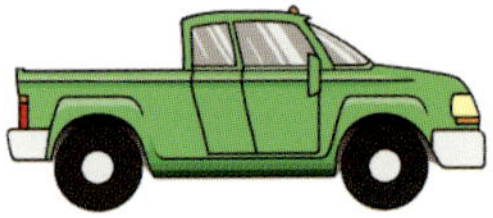 .

truck

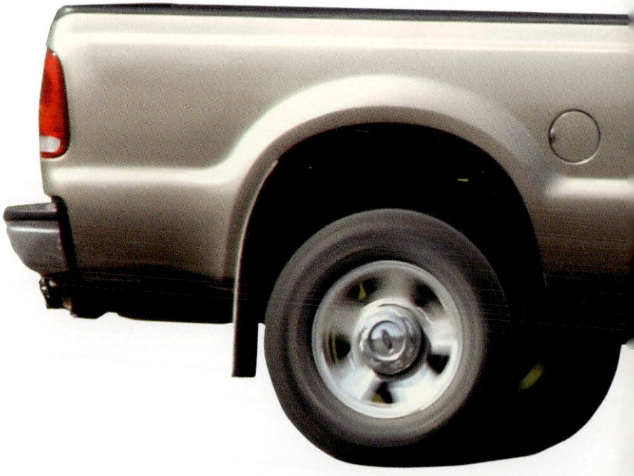

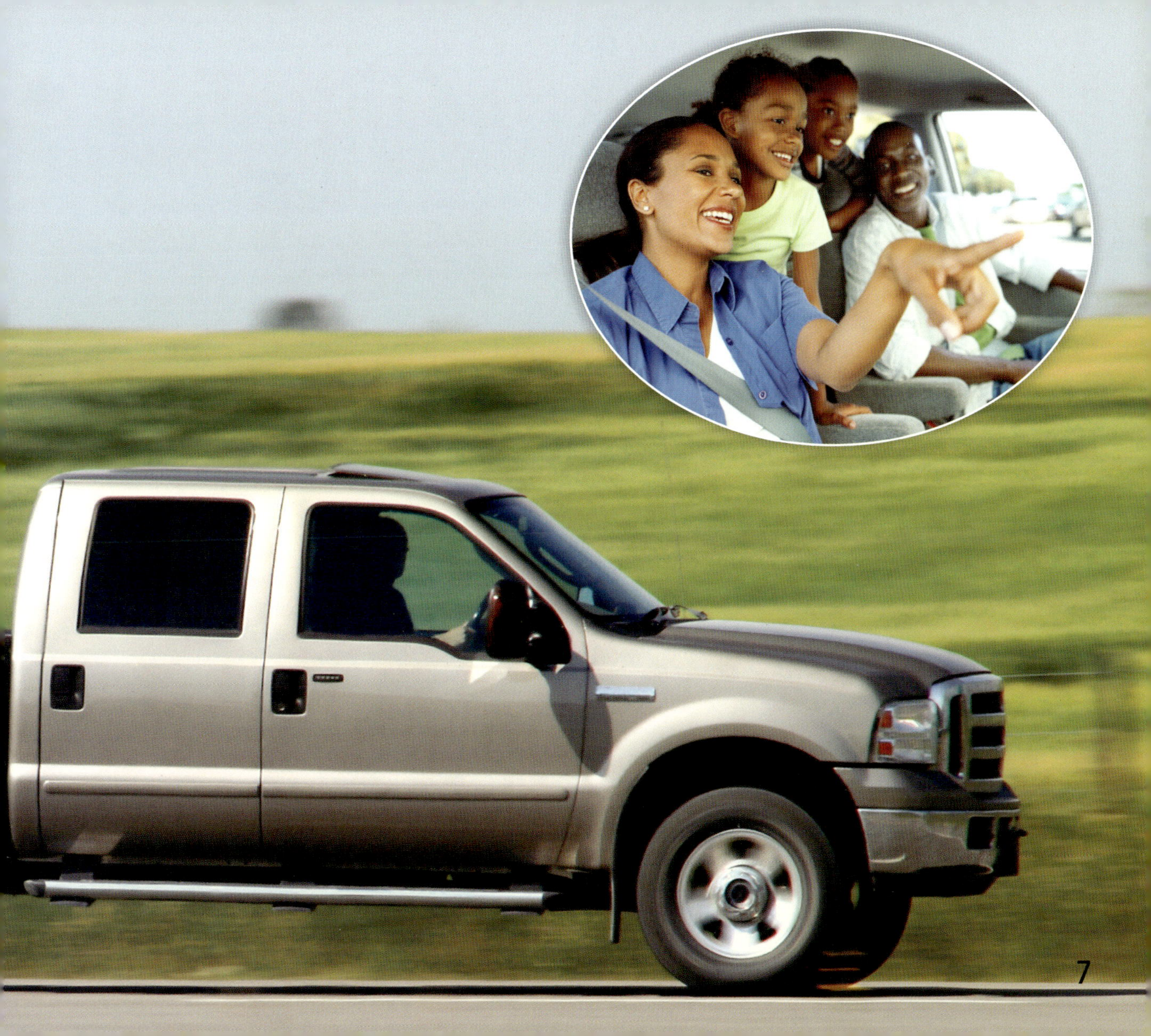

I go in a 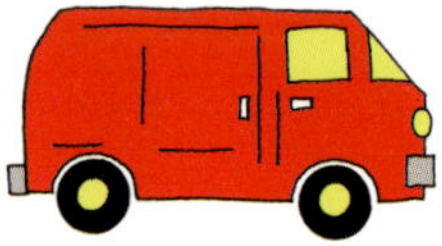 .

van

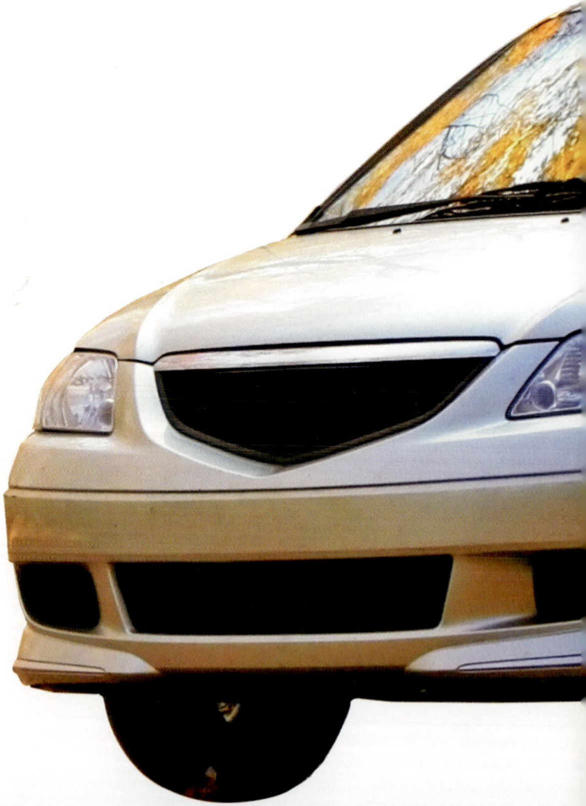

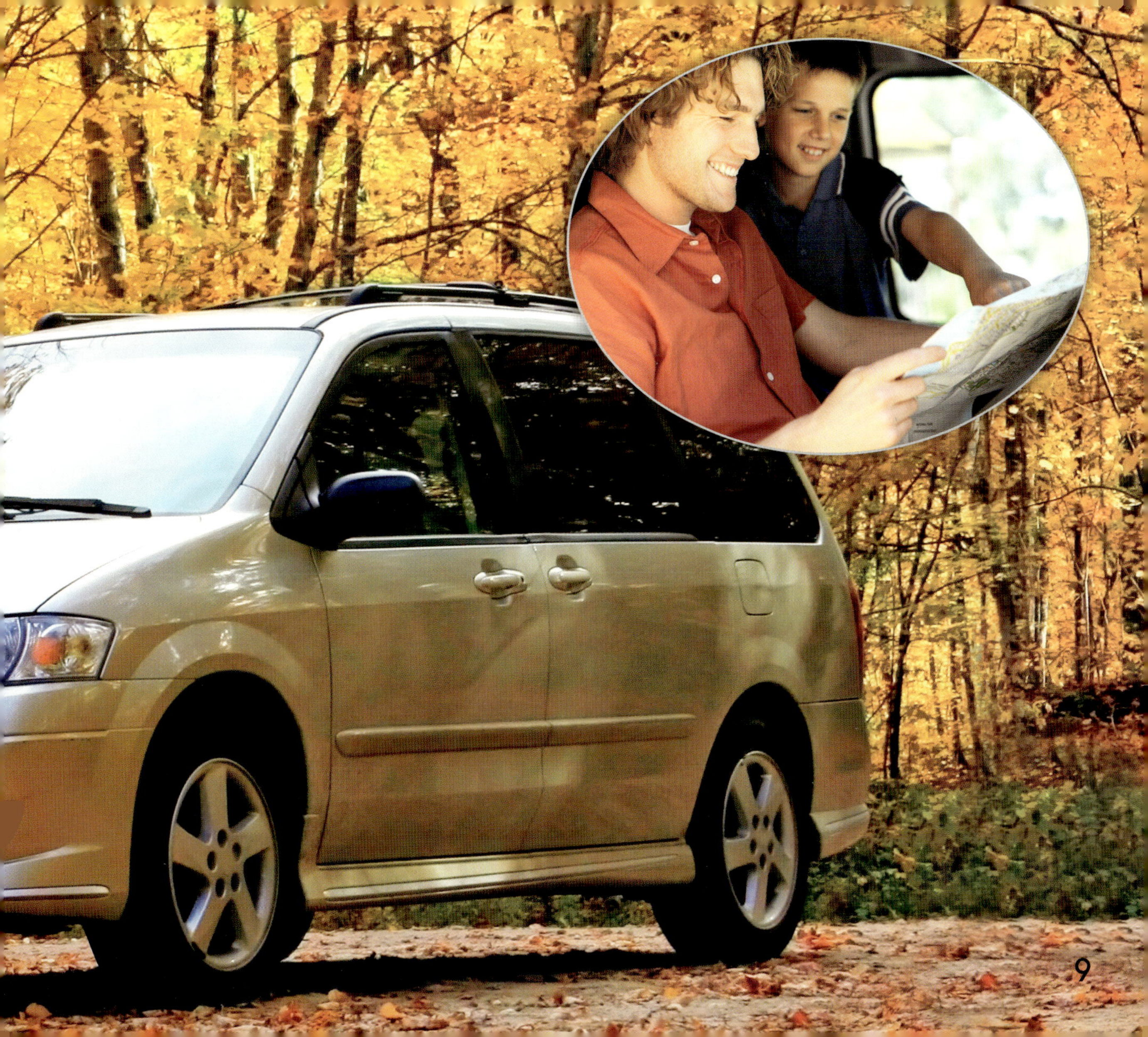

I go in a 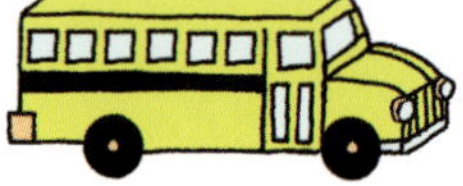 .

bus

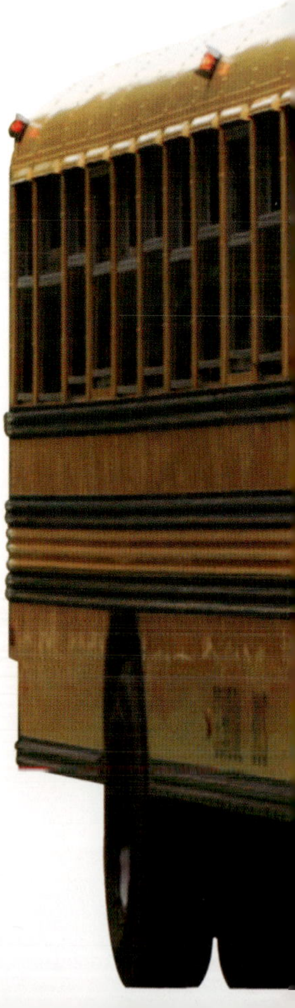